MW01102487

GL
IL NF
LX

We Need Zoo Keepers

by Lisa Trumbauer

Consulting Editor: Gail Saunders-Smith, Ph.D.

Consultant: Brandie Smith
Assistant Director, Conservation and Science
American Zoo and Aquarium Association

Pebble Books

an imprint of Capstone Press
Mankato, Minnesota

Pebble Books are published by Capstone Press
151 Good Counsel Drive, P.O. Box 669, Mankato, Minnesota 56002
http://www.capstone-press.com

© 2003 by Capstone Press. All rights reserved.
No part of this publication may be reproduced in whole or in part,
or stored in a retrieval system, or transmitted in any form or by any means,
electronic, mechanical, photocopying, recording, or otherwise,
without written permission of the publisher.
For information regarding permission, write to Capstone Press,
151 Good Counsel Drive, P.O. Box 669, Dept. R, Mankato, Minnesota 56002.
Printed in the United States of America

1 2 3 4 5 6 08 07 06 05 04 03

Library of Congress Cataloging-in-Publication Data
Trumbauer, Lisa, 1963–
    We need zoo keepers / by Lisa Trumbauer.
    p. cm.—(Helpers in our community)
    Summary: Simple text and photographs present zoo keepers and their role
in the community.
    Includes bibliographical references (p. 23) and index.
    ISBN 0-7368-1651-8 (hardcover)
    1. Zoo keepers—Juvenile literature. [1. Zoo keepers. 2. Occupations.] I. Title.
II. Series.
QL50.5 .T78 2003
636.088′9′023—dc21
                                                                2002014766

Note to Parents and Teachers

The Helpers in Our Community series supports national social studies standards for units related to community helpers and their roles. This book describes and illustrates zoo keepers. The photographs support early readers in understanding the text. This book also introduces early readers to subject-specific vocabulary words, which are defined in the Words to Know section. Early readers may need assistance to read some words and to use the Table of Contents, Words to Know, Read More, Internet Sites, and Index/Word List sections of the book.

Table of Contents

Zoo keepers work in zoos.

Zoo keepers take
care of many kinds
of wild animals.

Zoo keepers make sure animals have a clean and safe place to live.

Zoo keepers give food and water to animals.

Zoo keepers help
animals play and learn.

Zoo keepers help young animals grow.

Zoo keepers make sure animals are healthy.

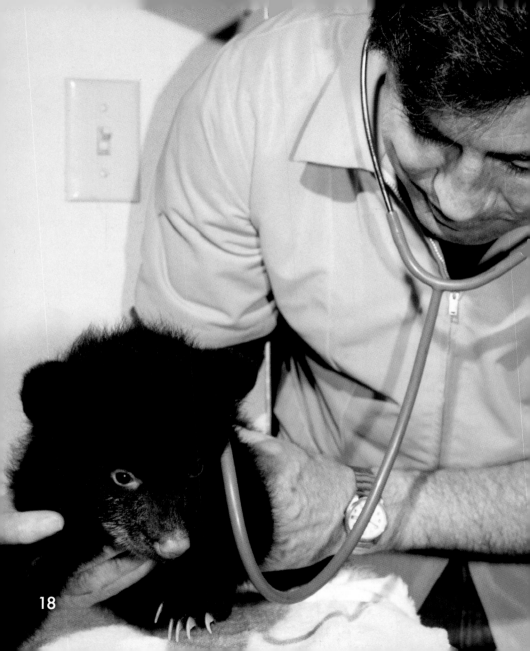

Zoo keepers
help veterinarians
take care of sick animals.

Zoo keepers teach people about wild animals.

Words to Know

grow—to become bigger in size; zoo keepers help young animals grow and become healthy.

healthy—fit and well

teach—to give a lesson or show people how to do something; zoo keepers teach people about zoo animals; they help people learn about animals from all around the world.

veterinarian—a doctor who treats sick or injured animals; veterinarians also check animals to make sure they are healthy.

wild—natural and not tamed by people

zoo—a place where wild animals are kept for people to see and learn about them

Read More

Deedrick, Tami. *Zoo Keepers.* Community Helpers. Mankato, Minn.: Bridgestone Books, 1998.

Miller, Heather. *Zookeeper.* This Is What I Want to Be. Chicago: Heinemann Library, 2002.

Schomp, Virginia. *If You Were a . . . Zookeeper.* New York: Benchmark Books, 2000.

Internet Sites

Track down many sites about zoo keepers.
Visit the FACT HOUND at *http://www.facthound.com*

IT IS EASY! IT IS FUN!

1) Go to *http://www.facthound.com*

2) Type in: 0736816518

3) Click on "FETCH IT" and FACT HOUND will find several links hand-picked by our editors.

Relax and let our pal FACT HOUND do the research for you!

23

Index/Word List

animals, 7, 9, 11, 13, 15, 17, 19, 21
care, 7, 19
clean, 9
food, 11
give, 11
grow, 15
healthy, 17
help, 13, 15, 19
kinds, 7
learn, 13
live, 9
many, 7
people, 21
place, 9
play, 13
safe, 9
sick, 19
take, 7, 19
teach, 21
veterinarians, 19
water, 11
wild, 7, 21
work, 5
young, 15

Word Count: 72
Early-Intervention Level: 8

Editorial Credits
Mari C. Schuh, editor; Abby Bradford, Bradfordesign, Inc., series designer; Molly Nei, book designer; Karrey Tweten, photo researcher

Photo Credits
American Zoo and Aquarium Association, 1
Corbis/Gail Mooney, cover; Dave G. Houser, 6 (upper left), 20; AFP Photo/John G. Mabanglo, 6 (lower right)
James P. Rowan, 4, 8, 10, 12, 14, 16
Visuals Unlimited/Ron Spomer, 18

School District 414
Deer Park
Elementary School
Library